T0088978

Also by Emma

Morning Messages

Heart's Messages
Messages from the Heart

Emma Gruzlewski

BALBOA.
PRESS

A DIVISION OF HAY HOUSE

Balboa Press books may be ordered through booksellers or by contacting:

Balboa Press
A Division of Hay House
1663 Liberty Drive
Bloomington, IN 47403
www.balboapress.com.au
1 (877) 407-4847

Because of the dynamic nature of the Internet, any web addresses or
links contained in this book may have changed since publication and
may no longer be valid. The views expressed in this work are solely those
of the author and do not necessarily reflect the views of the publisher,
and the publisher hereby disclaims any responsibility for them.

The author of this book does not dispense medical advice or prescribe the use
of any technique as a form of treatment for physical, emotional, or medical
problems without the advice of a physician, either directly or indirectly. The
intent of the author is only to offer information of a general nature to help
you in your quest for emotional and spiritual well-being. In the event you use
any of the information in this book for yourself, which is your constitutional
right, the author and the publisher assume no responsibility for your actions.

Any people depicted in stock imagery provided by Thinkstock are
models, and such images are being used for illustrative purposes only.
Certain stock imagery © Thinkstock.

Print information available on the last page.

ISBN: 978-1-4525-3155-7 (sc)
ISBN: 978-1-4525-3156-4 (e)

Balboa Press rev. date: 04/06/2016

Tony, you always see me for me, the real me. Thank you for being my twin flame.

And to you, all of you, always my beloved family, thank you; you bless me every day.

Preface

Again I find my fingers flitting across the keys to bring you more of the messages I find in the morning. With this collection of 150 messages, I've made a special book for you to open at random to find the message specific to your moment. May you find peace among these pages, and may the words touch your heart as they have touched the hearts of their recipients each morning.

When angels sing to herald the birth of a brand-new day, they again paint the sky with elegant beauty and colourful hue. See the beauty of colour in your life, in the painting of a stranger's smile. Give thanks for the joy of being able to see, and share this experience with all.

The greatest gift you can give yourself is a nourishing night's sleep. The greatest gift you can give others is soul-nourishing love. Give gifts that nourish, and see people grow and evolve.

The wings of angels stir the air and move us all to ease and grace as the dawn makes her way across all faces. Turn your face to the sun, and feel angelic warmth sweep through you.

May your day be blessed with sunshine and warmth. Be in love and graceful ease; may God keep you today.

Golden kisses cross the sky; may peace and love shine for all today. May your day be blessed and filled with love.

As angels flock and congregate, inspiration spreads its wings. Be open, receive divine guidance, and share it with your peers.

Through golden smiles and love abundant may all your heart's desires be realized. May angels always be at your call, and may you find your peace within.

Lights start to dance as God's scenery begins to change to the freshness of a new dawn filled with joy and peace. Dance as you spread your light of love today, and feel the peace of joy.

Earth Mother moves to support you in love and peace today. May the blessings of today be yours to hold close to your heart.

Angels sing and dance in dawn's first light and morning rain. Childlike fun brings all closer to God space, so dance, love, and jump in puddles today.

Let the light of peace and love shine brightly throughout your very being; be the angelic being you are. Smile with your soul at peace and know that love is the eternal flame that shows all the way to grace.

May today be filled with love, peace, and joy for you. May the gifts in the beauty of a sunrise be a blessing to your day.

God's light in early morn warms angels' wings to fly with love and spread their light across the world. As you love, remember to fly today.

Morning light peeks over the horizon, twinkling with new opportunities. Twinkle today and be another opportunity to the world.

With infinite love and gratitude may today be
as you make it. May love hold your hand, and
with light for your path, may you find peace
within.

Earth warms her feet and lands as dawn's light appears. Be warmth to the world, and spread your healing love.

Love life and live in the light; it shines for you and me. Be a light and a guiding hand, knowing your soul purpose is complete.

Hold hands and gently help guide all through tranquillity into grace's eternal loving arms. Angels light the way with souls aflame with compassion and peace. Breathe gently through the process, and know all is as it should be.

God's grace is in every new dawn, peace and love in every birdsong. Be peace, love, and grace as you move throughout your day.

Angels skip and play as they bring forth another day, to be filled with the gifts of love and light. Be an angel sharing the gifts, and see more souls skipping with exuberance and peace.

As the sun rises in beauty's abundance I send
you light and love. Opportunity abounds in the
rising of the sun. Seek your way with love.

Angels sing with hearts of peace and joy.
Remember to sing with love and peace today.

Peace and beauty of morning's light follow you through your day. Early dawn and birdsong create a peaceful morn.

As dawn appears in colours rich of gold, we love and laugh and share. This is our gold to spread around the world.

A golden dawn kisses in greeting another new day. You radiate healing earth energy. Shine and send it out into the universe.

Always look to the golden dawn; the way ahead is glowing. To reach the highest peak in life means you are always growing. As angels soar so too do you, for you are an angel without wings on show. Remember who you truly are, and give thanks that you now know.

Dawn glows a warming shade with peace and love for another day. Gold twinkles in dawn's kisses as she sweeps across the sky. Be as gold and twinkle your love as your beautiful day unfolds.

The new dawn starts to weave her daily web
in graceful sways and lines. Be as the weaver
in your life and show all how to bring love in.

Treasures abound in dawn's first light. Know you are a precious jewel kissed afresh with each new dawn.

Love heals in the kindest way; tears do cleanse the soul. Be open to true and lasting healing today, and know your soul is gold.

The earth is warm with the sense of love that fills every heart and soul. Remember today is love.

As the sun greets another day with love and peace, send forth your love and peace as healing to the world.

Angels bring love in the freshness of the new day to fill the gaps with joy and light. Send your love as a wave before you to fill the gaps with peace so your steps may continue to be loving and kind as you walk through your sacred journey.

Close your eyes and take a deep breath, and when you open them seek out a surprise. The surprise of realization and angelic manifestation works for you as me. See the surprise gift of every moment, take a breath, and breathe in infinite love and gratitude.

Love and joy and peace prevail when we steer
our hearts true. Keep looking toward the light
in life, and all good things will come.

As the angels change God's scene to that of a brand-new day, we remember to change the scenes in our own lives to see love and joy everywhere for all.

God waves his hand, and the scene changes to beautiful glory and fresh hope held in the light of a new day. Be glory and light today, and greet all with love.

Dawn's light carried on angels' wings spread warmth and love as they go. Spread your light and love to the world, and wrap it warmly around every heart.

The sun rises and sets, marking each new day, showing a clearing path. Greet each new day as a brand-new start, and forever love your yesterdays. Live in the moment, and be who you are now today.

Angels' prayers and heavenly hymns are sent to you from above. Feel the strength of a thousand men, and know this too comes from within. Never is a night so dark that light cannot be seen. Be the light, and see the light reflected back again.

Dreams filled with loving hope draw us gently into the light of a new day. Share your dreams with love, and joy and peace shall be surrounding with angelic embrace.

Sun rises as angels fly to spread love out over the world. Be as the angels and touch all with love.

As angels welcome a new dawn with colourful banners waving across the sky, we are encouraged to remember to spread our gratitude like flags blowing in the breeze.

With love, open your heart and soul to feel the ways of the world we know. Every day a new experience, every day with strength, all grow. To hold all in sacred heart space is peace on earth for all.

Be clear and ask if in need, for the angels are ready to hear your prayers. Be open in your heart to receive and know your answer is near.

Morning comes, the day begins, elders sing, and angels bring the messages of love and light for all today. Sing and be the love and light today.

Morning rains and God's love are spread to wash away all the worries of yesterday. Be love and light today, and spread fresh love to all.

After darkest night, always comes the most beautiful dawn, drawn forth by magnitude of angels for all to know peace and love. Shine your light into darkest corners, and see the love that hides there.

An awakening Ohm and morning prayer breathe new life into all everywhere. Spread your message of peace and joy, forever helping to heal hearts and souls.

Feel the freedom of surrendering into divine love; feel the healing and release. Be at one with the feeling now, and know your soul is pulling your heart into gracefulness.

God's trumpet in birds' morning song calls forth all hope and glory for the beauty of another joy-filled day. Send your messages of love and light today through every interaction.

Peace of the new morning brings hope of a love-filled day. Be peace-filled, and love with your all. Angels surround you always.

Another sunrise as beautiful as you has kissed the sky today. May all its magic be yours. Have an amazing day.

When all around seems to be in darkness, without a shred of light, look deep within your heart; it's there shining bright. Reach out a hand and grab another; there is no need to fear, for only is it from the bottom that we get to the top and cheer. Spread love and understanding. We all need to just be heard, to be a guiding light for all so the shadows can be cleared.

Refresh, relax, revitalise. Breathe, bless, be. Give gratitude graciously. Love life, live, learn. Help hands; hold hope. Share the lessons you've learned, and help others see the blessings in their lives. Be thankful always.

Morning song dawns across Earth Mother's face, leading from dreamtime into day. Dream and be led through your day, today, following the feeling of ease and grace with love.

Angels laugh as dawn lights the sky, spreading love in sweet reply. Shine and laugh and share your love as the angel you truly are.

Angels guide, and angels seek to help you find a happy soul. Spread the joy of your happy soul so angels can know their job is complete.

All of life is intertwined; all is giving and receiving only love. Look to the colour of the love that's shown, and use it as a guide to heal. Be free in giving and receiving all colours of love, and navigate the waters to peace and harmony-tinted hues.

Wings flap, a new day begins. Mother Earth sends her love out from her heart to warm our souls. Warm each soul you touch today.

Morning's song has begun, and day's hope grows in peaceful steps. Love and remember today.

May today treat you with all the love your soul needs to shine. May today be blessed with the beauty and peace of the sunrise.

Shine your light, and the sun will follow everywhere you go. Have a beautiful day blessed with angelic moments.

May peace, love, and eternal joy be your blessings today. Feel it there in your very being, and shine as the brightest star.

Earth Mother and Sky Father dance along to their own beautiful creation made of peace and love. See and show others, with love, the glory that is our beautiful gift of home.

Morning sun rises with peace and love. I send these to you with love and light.

Angelic grace brings a new dawn with love, joy, and peace, a message for all. Share your message of love so all can see your angelic grace.

The laughter of angels is heavenly delight. The laughter of happy souls is angelically divine. Find the pure happiness within your heart, and let your spirit soar. The angels and heaven are awaiting the divine sound of your laughing call.

Spend time exploring the natural world today.
Take a walk, admire a butterfly, stare at the
wide blue sky. Whatever you do, large or small,
angels aim to delight you with wonder.

Dawn's grace and God's love warm every new day. Warm the hearts of all you meet, and grace will be your guide.

Morning song of birds at dawn carries forth a brand-new day. Keep a song in your heart, and sing with joy.

Night moves seamlessly into day with softest threads of angels' song. Dark changes to early morn, full of promises of love and true glory. Shine your light of love, and let glory be yours in every smile.

Be within yourself today, and lovingly find your centre. Talk to your inner spirit, and listen for all you may learn. The union of you with your heart and soul is more precious than any jewels or gold.

Feeling peaceful with the angels is release; breathe with ease and grace. All is as is needed, and love is all there is. Find the joy and sunshine within your heart, and aim to illuminate the world. Hearts and souls rejoice in this as all our prayers are heard.

Dawn appears to clear the way for a bright, new, and exciting day. See our earth mother, and shine your love over the world.

Angels sing with love in the air of early morning. Sing your song of love today, and sing it loud and strong.

As your fairy skips amazingly, I hope you do too. Have a fairy, magical day.

Let go of all that hurts and hold only love within, for you are a champion in the new world. Be ready to show others who are ready the way back to their heart, and give thanks for angelic support.

Peace goes where love flows with angels lighting the way. Change is here, so give a cheer, and follow your heart to bliss.

Hearts beat in time with Earth Mother's rhythm in loving harmony. Feel the love flow through you, from your soul to your crown, and send forth your peace-filled grace.

Dawn appears as God's first gift full of opportunity. Be as a gift to the world, and light the way with love.

Angels giggle when your eyes twinkle in loving reply to the peace, love, and hope you share with the world. Go forth and shine your light for all to see the angelic blessing of you.

At rainbow's end is the fabled pot of gold, glistening in its purity. Let the pot of gold in your life be to seek out the purity of heart and soul.

Love is a gift; it is free and grows stronger every day. Let your love grow strong and sure, free of any restraint. See your love as a mighty oak tree, and stretch your roots and limbs.

Birds are in song and morning dawns; Earth Mother sings in a brand-new day. Sing and love and shine for all to know you are divine grace.

Angels dance and sing as the new dawn moves across the sky. Remember to move with loving grace and dance through the day so others may follow your lead.

May the grace and peace of every morning follow you throughout your day. You spread your light out, and others will find their way to love.

With angels' wings and sheer delight we give thanks for all that is golden. Through hills of green and mountains too, wish happiness and healing to old and new.

When angels arrive in heavenly procession to help you with a vexing question, don't hold back, lay everything bare. Your angels are there because they care. As your troubles and woes begin to subside, hold joy in your heart and gratitude inside. Share your gratitude as a wave of love, for the angels have gifted you with healing from above.

The sun rises to give love to another day. Angels play at your side eternally. Be light and love to the world always.

God's embrace warms each new dawn to guide his light out over the world. Be as part of the sky, and help in sending it out far and strong.

Angels giggle with sweet delight at another dawn of earthly delights. Giggle with your angels as they lead you through your day.

Angels surround you in all ways. See your day as blessed in all ways.

Smile with your all today; smile from your soul. See the joy and beauty of life, and share it with all through a smile. Smile for the sake of smiling, and watch the world turn and glow.

Mornings come to trim the day in love and joy.
May we remember today.

Morning comes and seasons move on with love and peace to another place. Remember to love today as seasons move and change.

Peace fills the morning air with joy and purest love. Feel love surround you in every movement, and embrace today with your all.

Mornings are the sweetest time; all is fresh and new. Be as the morning with gratitude, for it will see you through. See a shower of loving light washing your soul clean. As the rain wets the grass, all breathes and is renewed.

Angels guide and angels listen; always are they there. Helping the heart or helping the hand, angels hold us dear. Feel them close and feel them in all ways; angels we are and always will be.

As Earth Mother changes her gown from deepest night to early morning, the fresh breath of new promise holds sweetly in the air. Be light and new promise to all you see today.

Love spreads across the land as the glory of God's grace sees the dawn arrive. Feel the freedom and warmth of God's love, and move with it into ease and grace.

Beauty abounds in the sunrise as it does in you.
Send love before you, and angels will appear
and surround you.

Surrender all your egos and judgments always
to your higher source. We have nothing but time
on our hands, so nurture our souls first.

All of life is made of taking one step at a time, and living in the moment with infinite love and gratitude in your heart for the process. Take each new step one at a time, and forever being filled with love as gratitude sees you through every moment.

Dew's kiss in early morn lights journey's road ahead with softest diamonds, each one another blessed step to take. Know you are blessed in every move you make.

In every dawn a new day brings peace, love, and hope for us all to share. God's grace abounds in every step, so walk tall and shine.

As angels soar they leave their mark like a sign across the sky. Leave your mark today to show the angel you are and soar as eagles on high.

As the sun rises to warm another day, know you are held in eternal love and are surrounded with healing peace. Angels are with you always, in every smile and in every heart.

As angels sing through birds' morning chorus,
we are greeted with a day most blessed. Share
the joy of your love-filled heart, and see the
angels' blessings grow and spread.

God's love in every stroke of dawn's colours shines love over the world. Be colour and love to all you meet today.

Dawn's rays spread like fingers through the sky, guiding us to share our love as we reach out to others.

May your night have been restful and your
sleep sound. May today treat you wonderfully,
with much love and light.

In the quiet of early morn, as birds chirp their dawning song, hearts can find peace in the stillness. Find the stillness within, and draw strength from there deeply. Know this is how you find the peace in your heart.

Good mornings are the sweetest thing; angels skip merrily along, blessing every new day. Share a good morning along the way today as you skip merrily along, blessing everyone you greet. Feel the love of a thousand angels as they hold your hand throughout your joy-filled journey. Share the joy of a love-filled heart, and your soul will be forever grateful.

The sun warms our mother's womb to bring forth our love for her. Give your love as warmth to the earth.

God's grace calls forth the beauty of a new day filled with peace, hope, and love. Call forth your peace with love, and hope will be that which you share with all.

A morning glow and an angelic embrace—
peace abounds in love's sweet face. See love,
and glow in peace and light.

Angels abound and keep you safe so you can be free to dream. Dream big and dream grand so angels can help turn them into reality.

When angels sing in harmonious chorus, the world is at peace. Sing your soul's song, and join angels in spreading their pure message of love.

Sister air breathes life into every corner of mother earth, clearing a way for love to move with ease and grace. Feel the grace of every breeze, and know it's filling you with purest love.

Dawn's light fills the sky, shining eternally peace, love, and hope for each new day. Spread your love out over the world just as light spreads out to connect us all.

Angels sing, and dawn begins. A new day of opportunity is here. See opportunity in every action so as to be the love and light in the room.

Morning suns blush across the sky's cheek is as pure and beautiful as the light in your eyes. May the peace and beauty of the sunrise see you in angelic comfort today.

As angels beam, proudly watching over us evolving souls, great shifts across the universe are felt. Shifts toward kindness and love and truth, in every heart and mind, are the greatest gifts our angels are guiding us to experience. Give these gifts to all you meet so they too can evolve, surrounded by beaming angels, experiencing and joining with all souls the universe over to become truly one.

Morning breeze shifts the air, clearing a way for love and joy as God sweeps away the bustle of yesterday. See today with clarity and joy for all you see and surround.

Dawn's first kiss and birds' first song spread light and warmth in the early morn. Be light and love to the world today.

Angels sing, a new day begins, and we are blessed again. See and be the blessing to the world.

With angelic grace and peaceful keep, surrender to your higher good. Be safe, and know you're always kept precious, for your heart and soul are treasures.

Spread the happiness that lies within your heart to all you meet today. Show all the way to be angelic love and peace through being a loving change.

As the new dawn leads the way with peaceful love and full glory, the elders begin a new story. Begin each day with a new story so all may remember their loving grace.

Peace abounds in dawn's first light and is carried in your heart.

With the rise of the sun comes more energy to seek peace and love. You have power beyond measure; claim your peace and love.

When infinite love and gratitude permeates everything you do, those around you thrive. Give freely of these lessons, and your soul will be forever peaceful.

By one foot in front of the other we progress and move forward. By one foot in front of the other our pain is slowly shed and falls away. By one foot in front of the other we grow and therefore can teach another to be free and happy again.

The grace of God's hand in every dawn's brush mark shows true love in every morning. Paint your world with grace and love for all to see the beauty of you.

Angels rise to sing and morning rains to wash earth and energy clean. Be love and peace to all today.

Dawn's first light is a rosy hue full of peace, love, and light for all to wear. May angels keep you in loving embrace as you share your light unto the world.

When you become the change you wish to see
in the world, others draw from your strength.
They see that they too can be that change, and
when this happens the whole world grows and
evolves. Always be brave and stand strong, for
this is your life, so live it fully.

Laugh and love and live life fully, always finding peace and joy. Rest when your heart and soul are weary; restock and recharge. Always aim your journey to the light, and darkness shall be only your shadow.

Morning rain and Earth Mother's birdsong
call forth the beauty of another joy-filled day.
Sing from your heart, and feel Mother move
through your soul. Sing blessings and love
to all.

New hope in the new dawn leads birds to raise the chorus. Sing loud your praises, and send out your love for others to be led to peace. Songs fill the morning air with strains of peace-filled melodies strummed by God's own hand. Fill every face with loving melody, and listen for their song.

Remember to skip through the day and smile as it is the best way to have an awesome one. May the sun shine in your life and your eyes, even if it doesn't shine in the skies.

Angels trumpet and herald a new and blessed day; give thanks, for it is golden. Spread peace with every step you take, and treasures shall adorn your way.

Blessings abound and angels surround; we each are gifted a special today. Give thanks for all the wonders you see and gratitude for every miracle we share.

God's grace shines in every glorious dawn,
displaying beauty and love in all it touches.
Feel the grace and glory of love today, and share
it with all.

As colours change and lace night with day, angels bring forth messages of love and ease of grace. Move with ease and grace, and love will be your message.

May your head feel clear and your day be great.
May the rain be as refreshing and renewing as
you need.

A golden smile and cherished heart are all we really need in this life. Shining smiles show trust and faith, and cherished hearts are our treasure.

Angels dance with endless joy to see our smiling faces. Sweep the clouds from your skies, and bask in the glorious sunshine of your soul.

The gift of love that resides within your heart is cherished by more than a few. Remember the amazing blessing you are, and see how much you mean the world to all.

Final Thought

If you enjoy my words and the messages held here, please feel free to head over to www.booksbyemma.com. I'm also on Facebook; search "Books by Emma Gruzlewski." I look forward to sharing more of my journey with you through my blogs and posts. I'd love to hear your thoughts and feedback.

Enjoy today and every day for the cherished gift it is. Love blossoms from the heart as we share the joy-filled passion in our souls.

Blessed be with infinite love and gratitude.

Printed in the United States
By Bookmasters